Launching Eagles

*A Christian Parent's Guide for
Training Children to Discover Their Own Path*

by

WILMA KIRK LEE

Launching Eagles
Published by Watersprings Publishing, a division of
Watersprings Media House, LLC.
P.O. Box 1284
Olive Branch, MS 38654
www.waterspringsmedia.com

For permission requests and bulk orders contact publisher.
Copyrights © 2019 Wilma Kirk Lee. All rights reserved.

No part of this publication may be reproduced, distributed, or transmitted in any form or by any means, including photocopying, recording, or other electronic or mechanical methods, without the prior written permission of the publisher, except in the case of brief quotations embodied in critical reviews and certain other noncommercial uses permitted by copyright law.

Scripture quotations marked "ESV" are taken from The Holy Bible, English Standard Version. Copyright © 2000; 2001 by Crossway Bibles, a division of Good News Publishers. Used by permission. All rights reserved.

Scripture taken from the New American Standard Bible, © Copyright 1960, 1962, 1968, 1971, 1973, 1975, 1977 by the Lockman Foundation. Used by permission.

Scripture quotations are taken from the Holy Bible, New International Version®. NIV® Copyright 1973, 1978, 1984 by International Bible Society. Used by permission of Zondervan. All rights reserved.

Scripture quotations marked "NKJV" are taken from the New King James Version. Copyright © 1982 by Thomas Nelson, Inc. Used by permission. All rights reserved.

Scripture quotations marked (NLT) are taken from the Holy Bible, New Living Translation, copyright © 1996. Used by permission of Tyndale House Publishers, Inc., Wheaton, IL 60189 USA. All rights reserved.

Scripture quotations from THE MESSAGE. Copyright © by Eugene H. Peterson 1993, 1994, 1995, 1996, 2000, 2001, 2002. Used by permission of NavPress Publishing Group.

Printed in the United States of America.

Library of Congress Control Number: 2019911454

ISBN-13: 978-1-948877-25-1

*Eagles Who Live
in the Turkey Yard
Can Still Fly!*

Table of Contents

Introduction   6

Chapter 1 – Creating a Nest   11
Preparation for parenting ideally takes time. Parents need to establish their relationship and learn to interact with each other before adding someone else to their home.

Chapter 2 – Eaglets!   16
The thrill of adding a child to a family creates so much joy – in all generations. The immensity of the task of being a parent is now a reality.

Chapter 3 – Eaglet Talk   20
The conversation of the home is important from conception to launch! Children learn more from things that are "caught" rather than "taught"!

Chapter 4 – Eaglet Nurture   25
Children must learn how to use all of their individual gifts and talents. Parents need to know "One size does not fit all".

Chapter 5 – Eaglet Identity   29
Too often parents seek to live out their dreams through their children – that is NOT God's plan. Each child is created in God's Image – not ours.

Table of Contents

Chapter 6 – Three Cheers for Eagles   36
Affirmation is a necessary component of raising eagles. Too often children are not acknowledged for doing things well.

Chapter 7 – Look Up!   40
The environment seeks to keep individuals from soaring. Since turkeys can't fly, they seek to keep eagles in the yard with them. Eagles need to know they can look beyond their location and soar.

Chapter 8 – Launch!   45
Parents need to stir up the nest, so their eagles can fly! It's a difficult transition for all, but oh so necessary! This is a parent's measure of success.

References   51

About The Author   52

Introduction

This is a book to encourage parents to raise children who live up to the full potential God has given each child. There are so many voices today who are **certain** they know the exact way to raise successful children. Well, there are principles to follow, but as Christian parents, we are only charged to "train up" children. Proverbs 22:6 (AMP), *Train up a child in the way he should go [and in keeping with his individual gift or bent], and when he is old he will not depart from it."* We'll get back to the individual gift or bent. Just a thought, isn't it amazing that the God who is not through with us yet, allows us as parents to train children? The dictionary states that *train means to control or guide towards a specific goal.* God created us all in His image, which means we all have the power of choice. Parents find out early that children **definitely** make choices!

Every parent wants their child to succeed. Media is replete with examples of parents holding children back in kindergarten, so they can be at the *top of the pack* in grade school. Some parents argue with school systems to ensure there is more than one valedictorian for preference in college admissions…the list goes on. Parents have become so competitive on their children's behalf, there's a new term for them, *helicopter parents*, a style of child rearing in which an overprotective mother or father discourages a child's independence by being too involved in the child's life: *In typical helicopter parenting, a mother or father swoops in at any sign of challenge or discomfort.* It's important for parents to realize a successful parent works themselves out of a job! Deuteronomy 32:11 tells us the eagle stirs up her nest. Her eaglets cannot be launched as long as she provides for them and everything is comfortable – she works herself out of the job!

This book is targeted to any parent who only wants the best for their child, and wants to see their child as a self-sufficient, accomplished individual. A parent who wants an eagle must challenge them to fly. Flying is not easy – nothing of value ever is! Parenting cannot be a popularity contest where the parent always wins. A parent who launches eagles is preparing their child to make the right choices without having a parent always watching and telling them what to do! The words are still true today which Ellen White spoke in the last century, "Men and women are wanted now who are as true to duty as the needle to the pole, men and women who will work without having their way smoothed and every obstacle removed." [1]

I guess I'm writing this because I wish this had been around when I was parenting my children. I truly learned with OJT (on the job training). Our children survived to adulthood – in spite of my ineptitude as a parent! I DID tell them I wanted to raise eagles – I just wasn't sure how I could do that. They were my experiment. I love them because they still claim me.

Parenting today is not for the faint of heart – it requires patience, perseverance and much prayer. Even with knowledge and exposure, the results are not always perfect. Christian parents have the comfort of knowing, they are only asked to train – God produces the results. Philippians 1:6 (AMP), *"And I am convinced and sure of this very thing, that He Who began a good work in you will continue until the day of Jesus Christ [right up to the time of His return], developing [that good work] and perfecting and bringing it to full completion in you."* So Christian parents can breathe a sigh of relief because results don't rest with them! I must admit, I'm glad I'm not parenting today – there are so many things to challenge parents in raising children to God's glory: computers, smartphones, Facebook, texting, just to name a few. I didn't have to worry about those things when my children were young.

Eagles fascinate me in the raising of their young. There are so many things that if we were to study, we humans might learn much about how to train children, who are entrusted to us, to fly. The Bible refers to *where* and *how* the eagle's nest is built. This is the home from which eagles are launched.

I would like to begin this book with an allegory on what motivates eaglets to fly. My thanks to Tom Reilly, he is a professional motivator for business leaders; parents are the motivators for the development of their children. Most Christian parents only want the best for their children and are determined to see them succeed. Parents who launch children ready for the challenges of the world, realize they must allow children to learn some things through failure, not rescue.

The Power of Attitude by Tom Reilly

The nest of young eagles hung on every word as the Master Eagle described his exploits. This was an important day for the eaglets. They were preparing for their first solo flight from the nest. It was the confidence builder many of them needed to fulfill their destiny.

"How far can I travel?" asked one of the eaglets.

"How far can you see?" responded the Master Eagle.

"How high can I fly?" quizzed the young eaglet.

"How far can you stretch your wings?" asked the old eagle.

"How long can I fly?" the eaglet persisted.

"How far is the horizon?" the mentor rebounded.

"How much should I dream?" asked the eaglet.

"How much can you dream?" smiled the older, wiser eagle.

"How much can I achieve?" the young eagle continued.

"How much can you believe?" the old eagle challenged.

Frustrated by the banter, the young eagle demanded, "Why don't you answer my questions?" "I did." "Yes. But you answered them with questions."

"I answered them the best I could."

"But you're the Master Eagle. You're supposed to know everything. If you can't answer these questions, who can?"

"You." The old wise eagle reassured.

"Me? How?" the young eagle was confused.

"No one can tell you how high to fly or how much to dream. It's different for each eagle. Only God and you know how far you'll go. No one on this earth knows your potential or what's in your heart. You alone will answer that. The only thing that limits you is the edge of your imagination." The young eagle puzzled by this asked, "What should I do?" Look to the horizon, spread your wings, and fly. [1]

1

Creating A Nest

*"The best security blanket a child can have
is parents who respect each other."*
– Jan Blaustone

A study of the eagle will provide some interesting facts about nest building. One of the first things I noticed was, although the nest is built when eagles first mate – it's continuously added to each year. We live in an era of *instant gratification* – we must have what we want, and we must have it now! I am often fascinated by young people who state their independence but want to live in their parents' home because *"I can't have the same lifestyle if I live on my own."* It appears parents are not raising them to be eagles because they have not learned to build their own nest.

Scripture states in Genesis 2:24 (AMP) *Therefore a man shall leave his father and his mother and shall become united and cleave to his wife, and they shall become one flesh.* When a couple is ready to build their own nest, they are to **leave** the nest they were nurtured in and start building their own. They can't build their nest in the existing nest; they have to have a place and opportunity to build their own nest.

Nest building is not an immediate process. If you have ever had the opportunity to watch birds build a nest, you realize it takes them weeks to build a nest in which to lay their eggs. They gather twigs, sticks, thread, anything that will add to their nest. The male adult eagles share the task of building the nest – it's not just the job of the female.

People need time to build a strong nest for the children they wish to launch. Nest building is important for children – this is where they learn to be resilient. Children who come from a home where parents have learned to work together and build a firm foundation are the children who can handle success **and** failure, which is a part of living and thriving in this world. *-Parents should calmly consider what provision can be made for their children. They have no right to bring children into the world to be a burden to others. Have they a business that they can rely upon to sustain a family so that they need not become a burden to others? If they have not, they commit a crime in bringing children into the world to suffer for want of proper care, food, and clothing. (Adventist Home, pg. 164)*

The nest is the safe place, shelter from all the storms of the world and a place to go when there is a need for recharging. The eagles build a nest and this nest serves them for years to come. They continue to add to the nest each year as they raise their eaglets. Some nests grow to be as large as eight feet in diameter and weigh over two tons! If the fowls of the air make this type of preparation for their young, how much more preparation should human parents make? The addition to the nest annually by the eagles gives us a lesson in the work that is necessary in building a home. It is not all done in one day, but a constant work to provide stability, consistency and permanence for the family.

Nelson Mandela was a profound man with an appreciation of home and family. One of the concepts he shared about parents and their responsibility dealt with the type of home they built. He was not talking about the bricks, mortar, flooring, or furnishings, he was talking about the environment parents create. He said, *"We owe our children, the most vulnerable citizens in our society, a life free of violence and fear." As parents it is our responsibility to create a home that is calm, and peaceful, where our children can be the unique individuals they are. They should be able to make mistakes without fearing being punished by us.*

A marriage needs time to "season" before adding children to the family. However, when that is not the case, parents need to realize the nest is the foundation. They are responsible for building and making the nest sturdy. Children need the security of a strong nest. *A home that is built with Christ as the foundation and the Bible as the Guide will provide the consistent, firm foundation children need to thrive. It does not require costly surroundings and expensive furniture to make children contented and happy in their homes, but it is necessary that the parents give them tender love and careful attention.* (Adventist Home, pg. 154)

Unlike eagles, humans have to build a nest that remains **after the eaglets are launched!** One of the things I determined early on in our marriage that we would have a marriage which did not totally revolve around children. I wanted to have a relationship that would increase its luster throughout our lifetimes. I think we have succeeded in that quest, and now we have a Renaissance Marriage. (That's really another book). Having this kind of relationship helps your children know how to create a marriage of their own, which continues to honor the Lord when they are launched.

LAUNCH QUESTIONS:

Is your nest built to last after the eaglets are gone?

What can you do to make certain your nest will last?

2

Eaglets

...I'm the One Who's on your side, defending your cause, rescuing your children.
Isaiah 49:25 (MSG)

It takes a while to build a nest. Eagles begin the preparation for eaglets at least 1 – 3 months prior to laying the eggs. The nest must be built in an area that will support the anticipated family. They look for a spot that is high, for protection from predators. They also seek a spot which is near water to make certain there is a food supply for the little ones to come. When the eggs, usually no more than three, are laid, both the male and female eagle take turns watching the nest for the next five to six weeks. Once the chicks hatch, they require near-constant attention and protection from the elements, with both parents now sharing the responsibilities.

Amazing! In nature, both parents are responsible for the caring and provision of children. The dictionary defines the word parent as a father or a mother! Today when the discussion turns to parenting, everyone looks at the mother. Yet, just like a nest should be built by the husband and wife, launching the eaglets requires both parents as well. The talents and skills of both parents are needed to prepare their children for a full, well-developed life.

Once the eaglets hatch there is constant vigilance. They must be fed and protected, and the adult eagles are never far away, particularly for the first two weeks. Think about the birth of a new baby – everyone is around. In some cultures, family members come and live with the new parents for up to a year to give support and assistance. Everyone is involved in caring for the new addition to the family.

New children are a lot of work. They require attention around the clock. God's plan for a child to have two parents makes the work load easier to bear. Babies need the attention of both parents. Yes, often mothers nurse and must wake up for every feeding – it's a blessing when fathers get up and go get the baby and bring them to Mom. One parent is not totally exhausted, and parenting is shared. An exhausted parent is not capable of providing the consistency needed to help children launch successfully. The preparation for launch begins prior to the birth of a child. The thoughts and feelings of the mother will have a powerful influence upon the legacy she gives her child. If she allows her mind to dwell upon her own feelings, if she indulges in selfishness, if she is peevish and exacting, the disposition of her child will testify to the fact. (White) -- {1MCP 132.1} Again, Fathers are necessary to help create an environment of calm and consistency for the Mother during her pregnancy. It always takes two parents to provide a nest for the eaglets.

There's nothing more frightening, exciting, exhilarating and overwhelming than holding that new baby in your arms for the first time. You look down and realize – **YOU ARE RESPONSIBLE FOR A LIFE OTHER THAN YOUR OWN.** Too bad these little ones don't come with an instruction manual. Actually, whether you are a first-time or subsequent parent, you STILL need a manual – since each child is unique. I thought I knew what I needed to know when child number 2 arrived – was I ever surprised to find this child was not like the first one. I was starting from the beginning again. Child number three was even more unique – I often thought if she had been first, she might have been an only!

LAUNCH QUESTIONS:

If you could design a pre-parenting class, what subjects would you include?

3

Eaglet Talk

"We all need a cheering committee and parents are a child's most important fans!"
Vivian Kirkfield

Eagles begin their "talk" with their chicks early in life. Every time the mother or father bird comes to the nest with food, they are "telling" their chicks they are loved. Providing for a child's needs in a consistent manner shares the message, *"You are valued. I care about you and love you."*

Parents often feel it's important to **teach** children all the things they need to know to be successful in life. This is a daunting thought! Who knows what another person, specifically your child, will need to be the best? Do I, the parent, have all the knowledge and skills to teach them everything they need to know?

The most important thing for a parent to know is that children learn more from what is **caught** than those things which are *taught*. The influence of the home is truly powerful, but not so much because parents sit down and teach lessons, but because of the behaviors shown by parents in the home.

When language is noted, it is often thought words are all that is important. Research has taught us *words* **and** *tone of voice* are a part of effective communication. Parents need to realize that the tone of their words has an impact upon their child - even before the child understands the words spoken. Did you know that by the time a child is two he or she has a vocabulary of 150 – 200 words?

Researchers have found that infants are able to distinguish between speech sounds from all languages, not just the native language spoken in their homes. However, this ability disappears around the age of 10 months and children begin to only recognize the speech sounds of their native language. By the time a child reaches age three, he or she will have a vocabulary of approximately 3,000 words. Researchers have found that in all languages, parents utilize a style of speech with infants known as **infant-directed speech**, or *motherese* (aka "baby talk"). If you've ever heard someone speak to a baby, you'll probably immediately recognize this style of speech. It is characterized by a higher-pitched intonation, shortened or simplified vocabulary, shortened sentences and exaggerated vocalizations or expressions. Instead of saying "Let's go home," a parent might instead say "Go bye-bye." (Kendra Cherry, *Everything Psychology*)

Parent talk is also important for the development

of high-flying eagles in how children are affirmed. Although children may not have the ability to respond in understandable speech, they are receptors for all language going on in the home. Discussions parents may have about the children are heard and a lot of time understood! Parents often compliment or disparage the **child** rather than the **deed of the child.** When misdeeds happen, and they will with small children, it is important to remember the child is **not** bad, the deed may be! Children absorb both words and the tone of voice when parents speak.

It's amazing how we limit *"talk"* to words! So much is shared in communication through non-verbal language: eye contact, proximity, gestures, touch, facial expressions, and THE most important non-verbal, **LISTENING!** If you want someone important to you to feel valued, listening says that you are all there and interested, says **I Love You** without uttering a word. I often say, *"Women need to be loved with their ears."* However, the longer I live, the more I realize we ALL need someone who offers caring listening. Remember, this is truly how love is **caught**, not **taught.**

Your House Is Bugged...

Yes, your house is bugged!
In every house there are two microphones per child —
One is each ear.
These highly sensitive instruments pick up the table prayers,
The hymns sung;
Ordinary conversations,
Incidental remarks,
Types of language,
A variety of words,
And intensities of sound.
These all absorbing microphones
Transmit all that they hear to highly impressionable minds.
These sounds then become the vocabulary of the child
And basis for action and reaction.
Anonymous

Sam Walton, founder of Wal-Mart Stores had some principles for business. Here's one that applies to parenting relationships: **LISTEN** - *to everyone in your family. Figure out ways to get everyone talking. (Paraphrase, mine)*

LAUNCH QUESTIONS:

Does your communication style encourage your eaglets to share honestly with you?

Are they confident you value what they say?

4

Eaglet Nurture

It's difficult for parents to see their children as individuals – not little clones of themselves. Many parents feel when they become parents they can correct all their mistakes and live out their dreams in this young child who was just placed in their arms. God created each of us in HIS own image! He gave each of us distinct gifts and talents to allow us to reflect His glory in the earth. Yet, He allows us to choose to glorify Him.

Nurture means building *resilience* into children. Parents tend to be protective of their children, but sometimes protectiveness leads to coddling. No good parent likes to see their child hurt, yet, there are some lessons which can only be learned through trying and failing! Let's look at the meaning of *resilience*. The Merriam Webster dictionary states, "An ability to recover from or adjust easily to misfortune or change" as the definition of resilience. Let's look to the eagle and see how resilience is built into the young eaglets.

During the incubation period, one parent is always on the nest. The nest is never left alone by an adult bird. The eaglets hatch, but they must use the *egg tooth* to crack open their own shell. This process can take as long as twelve to forty-eight hours! Once the eaglets hatch, a parent, usually the female, is always present! Eagles feed their young by shredding pieces of meat from their prey with their beaks. The female gently coaxes her tiny chick to take a morsel of meat from her beak. She will offer food again and again, eating rejected morsels herself, and then tearing off another piece for the eaglet.

While on the nest with very young eaglets, parents move about with their talons balled into fists to avoid accidentally skewering their offspring. There are dangers within the nest for the young eagles, but the adult eagles provide "eaglet proofing" by their own behavior. I guess this is what happens when parents cover all the electrical outlets with protectors and put locks on low-lying cabinets.

We saw the resilience beginning with allowing the eaglet to crack open its own shell. Children begin by developing their unique personhood early in life – sleep patterns, food likes and dislikes. If we watch, we can see this individuality come to life very early in our children's behavior. We begin to diminish resilience when we do not recognize each child's individuality and the ways in which it is manifested in their character.

Adult eagles learn early not to do for their eaglets' things they should be able to for themselves. Look at the feeding process, early on the adult provides shredded food for the eaglet to eat. By eight weeks, the eaglet has grown to nearly the size of the parents. Their appetite has grown correspondingly. Parents are busy day and night trying to feed their brood. By 10 – 13 weeks, the down has turned to feathers appropriate for flying. The eaglet can even be left in the nest alone!

The adult eagles begin the process of helping the eaglet fly. Instead of delivering a meal, pre-shredded and offered up, the adult eagles often fly past just out of reach, carrying delectable meals: a half-grown jack rabbit or a plump rat raided from a dump. Although the eaglet is hungry almost all the time, they are becoming more playful as they lose baby fat; sometimes, when no parent bird was in sight, they pounced ferociously on a scrap of prairie dog skin or on old bits of dried bone.

A parent flew by, downwind, dangling a young marmot in its feet. The eaglet almost lost its balance in their eagerness for food. Then the parent swung by again, closer, upwind, and riding the updraft by the eyrie, as though daring it to fly. Lifted light by the wind, it was airborne, flying – or more gliding – for the first time in its life. It sailed across the valley to make a scrambling, almost tumbling landing on a bare knoll. As it turned to get its bearings the parent dropped the young marmot nearby. Half running, half flying it pounced on it, mantled, and ate its fill.

Resilience is a part of the process of allowing a child to learn what their capabilities are and finding out how to stretch past the comfort zone to use them. Parents cannot ignore this step and expect their children to become independent, healthy, creative adults. Scripture tells us in Proverbs 22:6 (AMP) *"Train up a child in the way he should go [and in keeping with his individual gift or bent], and when he is old he will not depart from it."* It takes a lot of time, patience and consistency to train rather than **do** for a child. Yet, the results are so rewarding when children are trained according to their gift or bent – they can fly!

Sure, it's far easier to use one method for all the children in the family. However, in so doing we dishonor our God. **He** created us as individuals to represent **His** glory. When we fail to train our children *according to their individual gift or bent*, it is not about God's glory but our convenience. It's far easier to set a system in place and make everyone fit into that system. This does not mean we allow children to be disrespectful or willful, that is not honoring our God either. Children who talk back, do not respond to parental requests, do not respect other adults, and think everything must go their way have not been **trained up** in the way God would have them go – they are following another leader completely. This leader is the one who deals in rebellion and disrespect. Parents have the responsibility and opportunity to set their children's feet on the right path.

5

Eaglet Identity

Once the young eagles have fledged (to acquire the feathers necessary for flight) they remain around the nest for four or five weeks, taking short flights while their primary feathers grow and strengthen. Their parents still provide all of their food. The young birds, except for their color, resemble their parents but are nothing like them in behavior. They have to learn how to hunt, and they only have the remainder of the summer to learn. Higher predators are born with instincts that urge them to fly, to bite, or to pounce, but precisely how to do these things is another matter. Through months of trial and error, eagles acquire basic skills such as lighting on perches or swooping on prey through practice. Eagles practice with almost fully developed bodies, and so sharpen their skills quickly.

Does this sound like adolescence? Young people who are still dependent upon their parents for everything: food, clothing, shelter, spending change. Yet, these same young people don't want to be seen in public with those parents and chafe with the boundaries parents set. It's a time of crisis for everyone.

This is an important part of the child's development. This is the time when they begin to put together all the pieces of instruction, education, and rules the parent has provided and determine how they will structure their own lives. Up to this point, the child is a product of things done to them. From this time forward, the child must determine what they will do for themselves. This is the time when life goals are set. Those goals represent education, occupation, and faith choices.

This stage is similar to another stage parents remember with concern, the *tantalizing twos*. Those were the times when everything the parent sought to do for their child was met with, *"I can do it myself!"* The child did not want help with feeding themselves – remember the mess? They put their own shoes on – usually on the **wrong** foot! Parents, you remember this time well. As parents, we were excited about this phase because it meant our little one was growing up and becoming an independent person.

Unfortunately, this same quest for independence does not bring the same excited feeling when our teenager starts asserting, *"I can do it myself!"* As parents we sometimes feel as if all the things we have tried to teach, and share are being thrown away! It's not being thrown away just being adapted for use by the individual child to take forward into their life.

Erik Erikson, a development theorist, states the development task of adolescence is to establish a personal identity. This identity must belong to the child, not the parent, and it is comprised of the personal philosophy of life. Unfortunately, because the child does not have a lot of life experience, that philosophy is usually based upon fantasy rather than reality!

A child's task is to discover who they are as individuals separate from their family of origin, and to become members of a wider society. Parents often throw up their hands at this point and determine they can't do anything with their children. Even as children search for their personal identity, they need parents to be consistent and set limits for their searching behavior.

One of the first things that young people seem to challenge parents on – is their faith system. Parents need to realize, nothing can be more devastating than to hear a child say, "I know that's what you believe, but I don't believe that way!" Spiritual beliefs, faith, and worship choices are some of the easiest ways for children to begin defining themselves as individuals. Faith choices are usually very obvious and a point of divergence for child and parent. This is a part of the *flight testing* for the young eaglet. Notice, eaglets **look** like their parents, have feathers that are capable of making them airborne, but they don't know how to use this ability.

Faith is like that as well. For years, children have been told Jesus is Lord of the home. He is the choice of the parents for directing their and their children's lives, now the time comes…Who is the Lord of the child's life? It's scary to allow children to make a decision about who will be Lord of their life. What if they don't choose Christ? What if they decide they can run their own lives? Does this make parents bad? What will other people think? It's not easy being a parent who allows eaglets to fly!

What's the answer to eaglet identity? It starts early in the life of the eaglet. Parents must live what they preach. I know, you have heard this all of your life, but never is it more true than when raising eagles. Eagles learn through a process called *filial imprinting*, in which a young animal acquires several of its behavioral characteristics from its parent. Simply stated, the eaglet learns to be an eagle and fly by watching the parent. Imagine what would happen to the eaglet if the parents **never flew!** There is a Scripture that applies here: II Corinthians 3:18(KJV), *But we all, with open face beholding as in a glass the glory of the Lord, are changed unto the same image from glory to glory, even as by the Spirit of the Lord.* Children begin very early in life to note parental behavior. They may not be able to talk but they can absorb through their eyes, ears, attitudes, feelings, and behavior of their parents. If their religious beliefs are not a part of **all** their lives – if their discussions are belittling and derogatory, then it will be easy to discard parental religious choices when they are making identity decisions. Remember the identity is about a personal philosophy of life – one's religious beliefs are the foundation of their life philosophy.

Parents are challenged to allow their children the same freedom of choice the Lord affords them. The Lord does not coerce our devotion. He only wants our service through **LOVE.** I John 4: 17- 18 (MSG) *God is love. When we take up permanent residence in a life of love, we live in God, and God lives in us. This way, love has the run of the house, becomes at home and mature in us....* This is the identity God seeks to form in us and He allows us to experience His love, and **choose** to allow His love *to have the run of our lives,* and sometimes we don't choose! Yet, we want to demand that our children choose our church – not the Lord.

If we want our children to develop a life philosophy which is based upon our Christian values, then we must make those values desirable and real. We must *"Love the Lord your (our) God with all your (our) passion and prayer and intelligence"* (Matthew 22:37, MSG, words supplied). We will then follow the admonition given in Deuteronomy 6:7 (MSG), *Talk about them wherever you are, sitting at home or walking in the street; talk about them from the time you get up in the morning to when you fall into bed at night.* The question will be asked of every Christian parent,

*"What did they see in **your** house?"* Will your eaglets know **who** they are? Even more importantly, will your eaglets know **Whose** they are?

WHO AM I?

"You shall love your neighbor as yourself"," replied Jesus.
Matthew 19:19 (Phillips)

What do I like about me?

_____

_____

_____

_____

Things I don't like about me:

_____

_____

_____

_____

I AM IMPORTANT BECAUSE GOD MADE ME, AND GOD DOESN'T MAKE JUNK!

"The Lord is disappointed when His people place a low estimate upon themselves. He desires His chosen heritage to value themselves according to the them. God wanted them, else He would not have sent His Son on such an expensive errand to redeem them."
Desire of Ages, pg. 668.

6

Three Cheers for Eagles

Affirmation is a concept necessary for eaglets to take flight. After all, if an eaglet is going to fly there are many things to be corrected to make certain flight is safe and certain. Affirming means *to declare positively or firmly; maintain to be true.* Usually parental communication to children begins with *"don't"*, *"you"*, *"stop"*. You understand the direction in which this is going.

Here's where affirmation is different – since affirming requires a positive statement, most sentences will begin with "I" rather than *"you"*. Some examples might be:

- I notice you listened without interrupting

- I want to thank you for picking up your things without being asked

- I love you

- I'm sorry

Affirmation requires discipline – not for the child, but the parent! Since the natural human reaction is to just speak without necessarily thinking first, we blurt out words without calculating the effect upon the other person. If we are in a crisis mode (angry, tired, hungry, sleepy), we just want to get our point across. As a parent, we have to realize just as the eagle never starves the eaglet, but provides nourishment, parents need to realize their words provide nourishment to the child's self-esteem.

Eagles learn to fly because they realize they have the capacity to leave the nest and use their wings to soar just like they see their parents do. Children who have not been nurtured to realize they have the capabilities to become someone who reflects the glory of God in a unique manner become stunted in their growth, limiting their flight potential.

Affirmation is the opportunity to *catch your child doing something good.* We are quick to pounce upon all the **wrong** behaviors we wish to correct, but we seldom affirm good behavior. We act as if we are entitled to good behavior and we don't have to acknowledge it.

It's important to remember, *Negative attention is better than no attention at all!* If your child cannot get you to acknowledge their good behavior – because it **is** expected, then they will misbehave so you will at least know they exist!

Our words of affirmation become a part of the child

as they develop their personal identity. The feelings associated with affirmation are endorphin producing – they give a sense of pleasure. They also encourage us to go after the thing that gives pleasure. If you are an affirming parent, then your child will seek to develop a relationship with you and your value system because it provides pleasure. What parent would not seek to have the child's memories be based upon pleasant experiences?

Affirmation also helps us as parents to focus on behavior, not personage. When children do wrong, and they will, we realize they are human. Humans make mistakes; James 3:2 (NLT) says, *"All of us make a lot of mistakes."* We have received grace from our Heavenly Father, and we must exercise that same grace with our earthly children. We learn to share with our children through *"I"* messages, and we also learn to use our *"I"* messages to discuss behavior. *"I was disappointed when you did not finish your homework."* If our child values our relationship, they will be touched by the disappointment in the behavior.

If our children don't value our relationship, it really makes no difference whether we use affirmation or criticism. Criticism will cause a child to abandon all the things the parent holds dear without a backward glance. Affirmation, on the other hand, will cause the child to consider what their behavior will do to the relationship.

Words – Words – Words

"No, No" Words

You Never

I told you so

You Always

I don't want to talk about it

When will you ever learn?

How many times do I have to tell you?

I challenge you to make your relationship one of **affirmation**, rather than criticism!

"Yes, Yes" Words

You're Fantastic

I Need You

Please Help Me

I Did Wrong

I Feel

Give Me Some Advice

I'm Sorry

Thank You

I Appreciate You

I Love You

7

Look Up

Parents have to make certain their eaglets know they can fly! Watch what happens as the eaglets learn they can become airborne. Once most of their wing and tail feathers are developed, the eaglets can finally leave the nest. First flights usually occur at 9 or 10 weeks of age and are preceded by vigorous exercising and flapping. The chick will typically lift off the nest by facing into the prevailing winds and flapping. Sometimes the adults will force the eaglets to fly.

Often the first flight will be to the nearest branch above the nest. When chicks leave the nest they usually glide to a nearby tree or stump, returning to the nest tree frequently and continuing to be fed by the adults. At first the eaglets have difficulty landing on tree limbs. However, if they land on the ground, they need open space to flap their wings to become airborne.

Within one month after fledging, eaglets will soar and drift over the river. There are some eagles who prefer the comfort of the nest and they won't venture far from the comfort and safety of the nest. The Bible says in Deuteronomy 32:11 (**NIV**), *"like an eagle that stirs up its nest and* *hovers over its young, that spreads its wings to catch them and carries them aloft."* Parent eagles make certain the eaglet has to fly! The eaglet is not abandoned or shoved out of the nest, but the nest is made uncomfortable *"stirs up the nest"* and the eagle stays near to catch them if they falter.

Remember the eagle has been preparing the eaglet for flight from early on in its development. The eagle flying by with food, rather than dropping food into its mouth was preparation for the day when the eagle would have to leave the nest because they must care for themselves. Parents begin the stirring of the nest when they allow their children to accomplish tasks for themselves rather than *doing* the task for them! Just as the eagle's first flight is not soaring – the eagle is there for support. The eagle learns the sensation of flying by doing just that – flying!

Sometimes the eaglet does not have the model of a flying parent to emulate – then what? A story I found about an eagle raised in the turkey yard illustrates this best.

> *There is a story about a little eagle that fell out of its nest and landed in a turkey farm. The eagle grew up among the turkeys and, although he looked a bit different, he learned to waddle like a turkey, bob his head like a turkey, and act like a turkey.*
>
> *One day the young eagle looked up into the sky and*

saw a beautiful eagle soaring above. The little eagle in the turkey yard thought, Oh, I would love to be able to do that! As the eagle soared overhead, it looked down and saw the young eagle below. Suddenly it swooped down to the ground and asked, "What are you doing here?"

The little eagle replied, "I am just here in the turkey yard where I have always been."

The great eagle looked and said, "Spread your wings, boy. You do just what I do. Follow me." Then he flapped his wings and lifted off the ground.

The young eagle tried it, too. "Wheeee! This is all right!"

"See," the mature eagle said, "you have been living among these turkeys so long that you were beginning to believe you were something you are not! Follow me, and you will find out what you really are."

So, the little eagle began to soar and fly. He loved it. But the turkeys down below called out to him and said, "Hey, little guy, what are you doing up there? You belong down here."

"No, I don't," called the young eagle. "I used to belong there, but now I am what I was created to be. I do not belong with you anymore."

God created each of us with different gifts and talents. We dishonor our God when we seek to make the children who are entrusted to our training just like someone else! We have to make certain our children know they are eagles and they can fly.

We teach them to look **UP** – they learn their help comes not from their parents or anywhere else, but from the Lord. When children learn to look up, remember the eaglet thought he was a turkey until he looked up and saw the eagle soaring, they realize *"Higher than the highest human thought can reach is God's ideal for His children." (Education*, pg. 18) Children will also learn they are unique and able to develop those talents and gifts given to them by their Creator in a way that honors God.

Resilience, which is a part of eagle nurture, is important for eagles to realize: they can feel safe looking up for help from the Lord. When children learn they have Someone Who is always there and loves them, they can make decisions about **who** and **whose** they are regardless of the peer pressure around them. There does come a time in a child's life when they are determined to be their own person – remember that's normal. They just need to be imprinted with the knowledge they were meant for flight – not to be a part of the turkey yard.

We have the privilege to raise eagles to fly by teaching them to look up, rather than at the circumstances around them. They were created to fly, and they have wings to fly – they just have to work at developing the strength of those wings. When they determine what **their** dreams are, they can be confident of accomplishing them because they have experienced watching their parents soar! They will also realize God's promise in Ephesians 3:20 (AMP), *"Now to Him Who, by (in consequence of) the [action of His] power that is at work within us, is able to [carry out His purpose and] do superabundantly, far over and above all that we [dare] ask or think [infinitely beyond our highest prayers, desires, thoughts, hopes, or dreams]"*. Fly, eagle, fly!!!!

8

Launch

I came across some lyrics from the song, *Wings*, the other day which reminded me how powerful the model of parents is in the ability of children to fly. The lyrics say:

> *"Mama told me not to waste my life,*
> *She said spread your wings my little butterfly*
> *Don't let what they say keep you up at night*
> *And they can't detain you*
> **'Cause wings were made to fly**
> *And we don't let nobody bring us down*
> *No matter what they say it won't hurt me*
> *Don't matter if I fall from the sky*
> *These wings were made to fly."*
> (Little Mix, 2012)

We've nurtured, helped to develop an identity, affirmed, and directed vision upward – what's left? It's time for the launch! Launching eagles is one of the most difficult things for a parent to do. After all, we don't want to see them hurt, disappointed, or fail, and the only way to prevent that is to **not** let them leave the nest. Besides, who will you as a parent have in your life if your children are not there? Scary thoughts, aren't they?

Yet, eagles are **made to fly on their own!** It's true, eagles are not always successful in learning to fly – some statistics state 40% of eaglets do not survive their first flight. Yet, the only way an eagle can learn to fly is through months of trial and error, eagles acquire basic skills such as lighting on perches or swooping on prey through practice. Eagles practice with almost fully developed bodies, and so sharpen their skills quickly.

It's difficult for parents to launch their children. However, it's God's plan for parents to work themselves out of a job! Just as development requires recognizing each child's individuality, so does launch time. Some children are ready for launch far earlier than parents want to admit, and parents are reluctant to allow them the space for launch. Today's society speaks of "helicopter parents" - Helicopter parents are so named because, like helicopters, they hover closely overhead, rarely out of reach, whether their children need them or not. Launch does not mean children will make only good decisions and do everything perfectly. Launch means children are now responsible for their own actions and behaviors – good and bad. Children must suffer the consequences of their behavior. Just as the eaglet learns to fly through trial and error, children must learn how to negotiate life through taking accountability for their actions without rescue by parents.

Human parents, unlike eagles, don't have to just push their children out of the nest and leave them to their own devices. Parents change **their** perception of their role – they move from protector to mentor. They raise their hands and allow their children to exercise their talents and concepts of how to do better than their parents. You **KNOW** they think parents don't have a clue! Now is their chance to put all their wonderful ideas into practice. Of course, they will make mistakes – they are still human. Yet, the old adage is true: *We learn by doing!*

For parents launching their children, there is nothing more comforting than the Words of Scripture, Lamentations 3:22-23 (NLT), *"The faithful love of the Lord never ends! His mercies never cease. Great is His faithfulness; His mercies begin afresh each morning"*. Those same mercies the Lord extends to parents, He extends to children. It's important to remember **children were leant to parents from the Lord. Children were His first!** God has **NO** grandchildren. Parents can trust the loving Heavenly Father to provide only the best for our children which are His children first.

So, parents launch your children! You can stand back in amazement as you watch their wings unfurl and they soar into the sky. As parents, you can then mount up on your **own** wings and fly beside your children and view the wonderful vistas before you.

> ..."*But those who wait upon God get fresh strength.*
> *They spread their wings and soar like eagles....*"
> **Isaiah 40:31 (MSG)**

It's time to end this story. So, let's use the story which began this journey:

The nest of young eagles hung on every word as the Master Eagle described his exploits. This was an important day for the eaglets. They were preparing for their first solo flight from the nest. It was the confidence builder many of them needed to fulfill their destiny.

"How far can I travel?" asked one of the eaglets.

"How far can you see?" responded the Master Eagle.

"How high can I fly?" quizzed the young eaglet.

"How far can you stretch your wings?" asked the old eagle.

"How long can I fly?" the eaglet persisted.

"How far is the horizon?" the mentor rebounded.

"How much should I dream?" asked the eaglet.

"How much can you dream?" smiled the older, wiser eagle.

"How much can I achieve?" the young eagle continued.

"How much can you believe?" the old eagle challenged.

Frustrated by the banter, the young eagle demanded, "Why don't you answer my questions?"

"I did."

"Yes. But you answered them with questions."

"I answered them the best I could."

"But you're the Master Eagle. You're supposed to know everything. If you can't answer these questions, who can?"

"You." The old wise eagle reassured.

"Me? How?" the young eagle was confused.

"No one can tell you how high to fly or how much to dream. It's different for each eagle. Only God and you know how far you'll go. No one on this earth knows your potential or what's in your heart. You alone will answer that. The only thing that limits you is the edge of your imagination.

The young eagle puzzled by this asked, "What should I do?"

"Look to the horizon, spread your wings, and fly."

Are You Ready for Launch?

Parents who are preparing their children for launch, will have instilled the following principles that their child will be able to apply. Where are you as a parent on this checklist?

☑ Trust in God

☑ Commitment to Others

☑ Initiative

☑ How to manage Finances

☑ How to care for oneself personally, i.e., laundry, meals

References

Foster W. Cline, M.D. and Jim Fay, (1990) Parenting with Love and Logic: Teaching Children Responsibility.

Ellen G. White, *Testimonies to the Church*, (2010) Vol. V, page 406, Ellen G. White, Estates

Tom Reilly, The Eaglet's Dilemma, *Seedlings Blog*, 2012
Erikson's Developmental Theory,
www.simplypsychology.org
National Zoo, American Bald Eagle Information

Cherry, Kendra, 2010 *Everything Psych*, 2nd Edition, Adams Media, Avon, MA

Ellen G. White, *The Adventist Home*, (1952), Hagerstown, MD, Review & Herald Publishing Assoc.

Ellen G. White, *Education*, (1903), Pacific Press Publishing, Mountain Home, CA

Little Mix, *Wings*, Columbia Records (2011)

About The Author

Wilma Kirk-Lee graduated from California State University, Sacramento with a Bachelor of Social Work degree, with a concentration in families and children. She received her Master of Social Work from the University of Arkansas Little Rock. She has worked with populations from the aging to early childhood.

She currently directs the *Center for Family Wholeness*, **(CFW)** located in Houston, Texas. One of its goals is to model how churches can set up similar programs in their communities that develop collaborative partnerships with entities that seek to provide services to families in their local communities. She is one of the founders of the Greater Houston Healthy Marriage Coalition.

Mrs. Kirk-Lee also served as Director of Family Ministries of Southwest Region Conference for 12 years along with her husband. She was responsible for the development of a conference-wide Employee Assistance Program (EAP) for all Southwest Region employees. She has authored a handbook for family ministries coordinators, QuickStart for Family Ministries, at the local church level, published through AdventSource for the North American Division. She has published a curriculum for marriage, Marriage Is for Friends, used for couples in strengthening marriages in the African-American community. She also served as a consultant and trainer for the Head Start program in Region Six - Arkansas, Louisiana, New Mexico, Oklahoma, and Texas.

Mrs. Kirk-Lee has written articles for the *Ministry Magazine, Message, Leadership Magazine, Kids Magazine, The Social NetWorker and the Human Sexuality Journal,* a publication for behavioral science college instructors by Williams-Brown Publishing, She has contributed to Sabbath School supplemental books, and she has edited the 2nd edition of the Family Ministries Curriculum and other publications of the Family Ministries department of the North American Division.

Trainings and Certifications for Mrs. Kirk-Lee are:

- Licensed Master Clinical Social Worker, State of TX
- Certified Family Life Educator, National Council on Family Relations
- Trainer, Technical Consultant, Head Start
- WHO (We Help Ourselves), Child Abuse Prevention Facilitator
- PACE (Parent and Child Enrichment) Facilitator
- Marriage Enrichment Facilitator/Trainer

Wilma Kirk Lee

Mrs. Kirk Lee was born in Minneapolis, MN to her pastor parents, Augustus L. Kirk and Mildred Bradford Kirk. Wilma has lived throughout the United States. In 2000, her mother, Mildred Kirk, moved to Houston, Texas to live in proximity, she is deceased as of January 2016.

Wilma has been married to her pastor husband, W. S. Lee for over five decades. She is the mother of three, Anthony, deceased, he left a daughter, Brittany Lee Lineback, who is the mother of Davion and Malik; Adrienne Lee Jones, married to Carl Jones and mother of Samuel Arthur Jones; Amber Lee Williams, married to Christopher Williams, mother of Maxwell Augustus Williams and Miles Christian Williams. She enjoys reading, crocheting, and her love of the color purple is manifested in her daily wardrobe.

www.ingramcontent.com/pod-product-compliance
Lightning Source LLC
Chambersburg PA
CBHW052209110526
44591CB00012B/2140